A SKETCH OF THE LIFE

OF

EDWARD ABIEL STEVENS D. D.

By his Son-in-law

PRINTED FOR PRIVATE DISTRIBUTION

RANGOON:
PRINTED AT THE AMERICAN BAPTIST MISSION PRESS.
F. D. PHINNEY, SUPT.
1886.

In the interest of creating a more extensive selection of rare historical book reprints, we have chosen to reproduce this title even though it may possibly have occasional imperfections such as missing and blurred pages, missing text, poor pictures, markings, dark backgrounds and other reproduction issues beyond our control. Because this work is culturally important, we have made it available as a part of our commitment to protecting, preserving and promoting the world's literature. Thank you for your understanding.

THE writer was requested by the Editor of "The Indo-Burma Evangelist," to prepare a brief memoir of the late Dr. Stevens. The work grew into the following narrative, from which selections have been made for the columns of that excellent periodical.

It is with much diffidence that the task, even in this simple form, has been attempted. The writer feels the inadequateness of his effort. To quote the words of one, who was for many years associated with Dr. Stevens in missionary work,—

"No pen can set forth the beauty, the sweetness, the aroma, of his pure, true, gentle spirit, coupled with his great firmness and strength of purpose, a life so noble, so long, and so uniform in its high moral tone, so crowded with wise and unselfish work, so replete with all Christian graces, and so rich in culture, and in human virtue."

D. A. W. S.

EDWARD ABIEL STEVENS.

ON a tomb in the old cemetery on the Isle of Shoals, New Hampshire, U. S. A. is found the following inscription:—

> In the Memory of the
> REV. JOSIAH STEPHENS,
> A FAITHFUL INSTRUCTOR OF YOUTH
> AND PIOUS MINISTER OF JESUS CHRIST.
> SUPPORTED ON THIS ISLAND
> BY THE SOCIETY FOR PROPAGATING THE GOSPEL,
> WHO DIED JULY 2, 1804, AGED 64 YEARS.
> LIKEWISE OF
> MRS. SUSANNAH STEPHENS,
> HIS BELOVED WIFE, WHO DIED
> DEC. 7, 1810, AGED 64 YEARS.

Oliver, the second son of this missionary on the Isle of Shoals, was the father of the subject of this sketch. Going to one of the Southern states to look after the property of a brother, who had been lost at sea on a voyage between New York and Savannah, he became acquainted with Miss Eliza Sumner Winn, whose father having on one occasion, with the well-known southern hospitality, entertained a Baptist minister on his travels, was, for this service, rewarded by a suggestion that the Bible should be searched for proof-texts to support the distinctive tenets of Pedobaptists. To his great surprise and disappointment, after repeated and thorough research, he could not find that for which he sought, and fidelity to his convictions compelled him to become a Baptist.

The daughter, up to the time of her marriage with Mr. Oliver Stevens, and for several years afterwards, remained a Presbyterian. The action of her honored parents could not, however, be without its influence upon her peace of mind, and her prayer for a long time was, "Oh God, if the Presbyterians are right, let me not become a Baptist." It was not until after the birth in Sunbury, Liberty County, Georgia, January 23rd 1814, of Edward Abiel, that her views became settled. Soon after the christening of this, her fifth child, she, with her husband, from the sheer force of conviction, joined the Baptists. Not long thereafter came to the United States the startling intelligence of the change in views of the Rev. Adoniram Judson and wife, and of their occupation of Burma, as a mission field. His appeal to the Baptists of America to undertake the mission thus providentially thrown upon them, supported, as it was, by the persuasive eloquence of Rev. Luther Rice, whose views had undergone a similar change, during his passage to India as a missionary in a different ship, produced a most profound impression throughout the entire denomination.

Mrs. Stevens, as her answer to the appeal, called in her pastor, and requested him, on the behalf of herself and husband, to offer their baby boy to God, for His gracious acceptance, for the Burman Mission. Of this incident, Dr. Stevens was for the first time informed, when on a visit to the South in the Winter of 1875-76. Writing in his journal soon after the date of that visit, he says :—" This fact, as related by this lady, was new to me, although I had learned from both father and mother, that in my infancy, they had expressed a *willingness*, if God should call me, to give me up to that service. And it explains to my mind, why, at an early age, my interest was enlisted in that enterprise, resulting in my devotion to it, while, in a family of nine brothers and sisters who attained to maturity, no other one evinced any special interest in the work. I regard the fact as a marked illustration of the efficacy of prayer, and the acceptance by God, as in the case of Samuel, of special dedication to specific services in the church. Nor can it be said that the effect on my character and life, was the result of special training for the work by my parents or others, for my training differed in no respect from that of the others; and when I actually proposed to become a missionary, my parents evinced no joy from the fact, although they dared not, as they said, make any opposition to the proposal, for they remembered the word spoken when I was a child. I am satisfied, in view of my early exercises on the subject, that the Spirit of God wrought in me to prepare me for the work, and to ensure my entering upon it. Other parents, we know, have done the same thing with the same result."

In 1827, at the early age of thirteen, Edward experienced, as he believed at the time, the saving change, and was baptized into the membership of the Baptist Church at Sunbury, in November of the same year. During his first year in Brown University, Providence, R. I., he received new and clear views of justification by faith, which made him doubt the reality of his conversion at the earlier period. From these clearer views of justification, it might be literally said, he had peace like a river, which flowed undisturbed, through life. In 1828, the year after his baptism, he was sent to the North, to the home of his mother's sister, wife of Dr. H. J. Ripley of Newton, Massachusetts, under whose care he fitted for college. He graduated from Brown University in the class of 1833, and from Newton Theological Institution in 1836. On June 27th of the same year, he was accepted by the Baptist Triennial Convention, (now American Baptist Missionary Union), as a missionary to Burma, and in that connection, so happy to him, he lived but one week less than half a century. He spent the following year in his native State, going about among the churches to stir up in them a deeper interest in the great work of foreign missions. On the 5th of October, 1837, he was married to Elizabeth Lincoln, daughter of Calvin Haven a Boston merchant, and a member of Federal, now Clarendon Street Church. Miss Haven was also a niece of Heman Lincoln long the honorary treasurer of the A. B. M. Union.

On the 28th of the same month, with Rev. Messrs. Stilson and Brayton, and their wives, Mr. and Mrs. Stevens sailed in the little barque *Rosabella*, Captain Green, for Maulmain. The year before, this same barque had brought to India another party of six. Imagine the shock to this party of the succeeding year to learn, on their arrival, that one-half of the preceding company were already numbered among the dead. The prospect of laying down their lives at an early age in the deadly climate, as it was then reputed, of Burma, was familiar to them ; but to be greeted with such a report, the sadness of which was intensified by the intelligence of the death of three other missionaries, altogether six, whose names were familiar, and the report of whose decease had not reached America on their departure, sent a chill to the hearts of that youthful company. How different, however, for themselves, was the result, from what their most sanguine thought could have anticipated ; for, of that party of six, with the exception of Mrs. Stilson, who died thirteen years afterwards, in 1851, all lived up to the present year, when Mr. Stilson died in March, and now, Dr. Stevens, in June. Instead of one-half of the party passing away in a single year, one-half still remain at the end of nearly fifty years !

Mr. Stevens was appointed to the Burmese department of the Mission in Maulmain, and with special reference to the Theological School, which had been commenced in Tavoy in 1836, and which was about to be transferred to Maulmain. Dr. Judson, then twenty-four years in Burma without a return to his native land, was in charge of the Burmese Church, and Mr. Ingalls of the English Church. Mr. Stevens, while learning the language, assumed charge of the English Church, and from that time, with occasional intervals, until finally relieved by Rev. L. J. Denchfield of the care of the English Baptist Church in 1882, he gave a portion of his time to the English speaking communities, first of Maulmain, and afterwards of Rangoon.

After being engaged a few years in the instruction of Burmese candidates for the ministry, he became convinced that the time was not yet ripe for such an institution, the majority of those who gave evidence of a call to the ministry, being elderly men with families looking to them for support, who would find it impracticable to enter upon a systematic course of instruction. These, however, it was his habit, as it has been of nearly all the Burman missionaries, to gather into classes for Bible study, during the rainy season months, when itinerating among the heathen is made impossible by the continual rain.

After his return to Burma, in 1876, nearly forty years later, a most hopeful beginning of what Dr. Stevens designed should grow into a Burmese Theological Seminary was made, for the support of which funds placed at his disposal by a friend, were available ; and not a few Burmese preachers and pastors from different stations in Burma, refer gratefully to the benefit received from successive seasons spent in systematic study with Dr. Stevens.

During this first period of his foreign mission work, the pastoral care of the Pgho Karen Church in Dongyan fell upon him for the space of five or six years. His visits to this church could be only occasional, but it was his custom to remain a small portion of each year with them. He became deeply interested in the work among the Karens, and it was his privilege to baptize a large number in connection with the Dongyan Church. He partially acquired the language and was, at one time, very strongly urged by some of his brethren, to transfer himself to the Karen department.

During the absence of Dr. Judson in the United States in 1845-46, and again, after his decease in 1850, the pastoral care of the Burmese Church, and the general supervision of the Burmese work in Maulmain, devolved upon him, up to the time of his own return to America, which took place in 1854, after a term of sixteen years in the country.

Dr. Stevens considered it one of the blessings of his life that he was, during his early missionary years, for more than a decade intimately associated with Dr. Judson. His estimation of Dr. Judson's eminent abilities, and his often expressed admiration of the superior excellencies of his work, constantly increased, as he became more and more capable of judging of them. On account of a disastrous fire, which destroyed his books and manuscripts, on the night of February 19th, 1847, there are no journals of his early years remaining ; and it is an interesting circumstance that the only volume which is left, opens with 1850, in daily records of the last days of Dr. Judson in Maulmain, the embarkation for Bourbon, and his own frequent visits to the ship, while it remained in the river, accompanying Mrs. Judson, as she took her daily farewells.

Dr. Stevens very soon acquired the Burmese language, and attained to an unusual facility in conveying his thoughts with accuracy, and so as to be readily apprehended by a Burmese audience. His pronunciation was admirable. It was often remarked by Burmans that by those who should hear without seeing him, he would not be suspected of being a foreigner. Books prepared by him in the Burmese language, whether translations or original productions, are pronounced by Burmese readers, (and Karen also), as remarkably lucid. In speech, he was the " golden-mouthed ;" and in conveying niceties of thought, whether in speech or writing, he was unsurpassed. In the latter, he was a worthy successor of Dr. Judson. It was to Mr. Stevens that Dr. Judson committed for completion and publication, the manuscripts of his Burmese Dictionary, which was issued from the Press in 1852, after the death of its distinguished author.

At the urgent request of J. R. Colvin, Esq., then Commissioner of Tennasserim, Mr. Stevens translated, for the use of schools, from the " Instructor," the " Elements of General History," in two volumes octavo, aggregating upwards of 400 pages. Besides a number of tracts, some of which have been and still are very much in request, Dr. Stevens prepared commentaries on Matthew, Romans, Galatians, and Hebrews, the only commentaries on the Scriptures ever printed in the Burmese language, a translation of Dr. Barth's " Church History," and a small volume entitled " Scripture Lands." In addition to the above, the " Religious Herald," a monthly paper now called " The Burman

Messenger," was commenced by him, in association with others, in 1842, and sustained by his almost unassisted efforts, while in the country, until his last illness. Indeed, one number, he prepared and issued, during that illness.

The Burmese Hymn-book contains eighty-four hymns bearing his initials. Many of these are translations of hymns dear to all Christians who sing in the English tongue, such as,

> "Rock of ages cleft for me,"
> "There is a fountain filled with blood,"
> "My dear Redeemer and my Lord,"
> "Jesus, Lover of my soul,"
> "Jerusalem the golden,"
> "All hail the power of Jesus' name," etc.,

The proofs of this hymn-book, in its many editions, as well as many editions of the New Testament, one with references, were corrected by him, as they passed through the press. For the last thirty years, few pages in Burmese have left the Mission Press, whether tract, Bible, text-book, or periodical, which had not been submitted to his scrutiny one or more times. A Concordance on the whole Bible, on which Dr. Stevens had been working at intervals of leisure for many years, was completed in 1880. Indeed, it was only at intervals of so-called leisure, that all this literary work was accomplished. Dr. Stevens was not what could be called a man of " the study," during any portion of his long career. It was as a preacher, a pastor, a teacher, and an itinerant, that he impressed himself upon those among whom he labored.

The secret of the amount of literary work which he was able to accomplish, was his methodical and indefatigable industry. He was blessed, too, with a temperament of remarkable evenness; he was not easily ruffled or confused by the pressure of a variety of demands urging themselves upon him at the same moment. In no other way can we understand how, for a succession of years, he bore burdens which would have crushed almost any other two men.

Soon after his return to Burma, in 1857, and his settling in Rangoon, he was invited to become the pastor of the recently established Church of English-speaking Baptists. In connection with this pastorate which continued uninterrupted until 1874, and which was resumed again in 1877, Dr. Stevens was in the habit of preaching Sabbath evening, of conducting a prayer-meeting on Wednesday evening, and of visiting the sick, the dying, the bereaved, the backslidden. Less than this he would not do and more he could not, without encroaching on what he ever kept before him as his chief and chosen occupation in Burma, the evangelizing of the heathen and the building up of the native churches. Indeed, the care of the English Church he ever regarded as only an incidental, though very precious and important service, which the Providence of God made incumbent upon him.

For several years of this time, Dr. Stevens was also Mission Treasurer, a work the onerousness of which can be understood only by those who have tried it.

During the rainy seasons, four and a half days of every week were given to the instruction of preachers' and assistants' classes, and the dry seasons to itinerating among the villages. This he was enabled to do by the uniform kindness of his brethren in supplying the pulpit of the English Church, during his absence. Nor, should it be said, was it only when Dr. Stevens was absent from town, that his brethren assisted him in the English pulpit. Those whose business brought them from other stations to Rangoon, were most cordial in giving him an evening of rest, and the congregation the benefit of a change of voice. For periods, too, longer or shorter, his missionary brethren in Rangoon would divide with him, the work of preaching. To Dr. Binney and Dr. Rose, the Rangoon Church was especially indebted during successive years, for sharing that service with Dr. Stevens. The intervals of home-coming were crowded with arrears of proof-reading, and editing, and the duties of his office as Mission Treasurer. Besides all the above, a Tamil and Telugu Church had been growing up in connection with the English work. This was subsequently organized in 1880, with ninety members, into a distinct body, and this new Church and its pastor, continued to look to him as their guide. It is no wonder that under such a constant pressure, the overtaxed system should rebel. In 1873, he experienced the first of a series of attacks, at first with long intervals, and towards the end more frequent, the last of which in complication with heart trouble, hastened his decease in 1886.

In 1874, after a second term of service which consisted of eighteen years in Burma, he felt the need of change and rest, and in March of that year, he turned his face homeward to make his second and last visit to his native land. It was his privilege to leave behind him in Burma a son and a daughter, who had already been engaged for several years in mission work in their respective stations of Prome and Henthada.

During his two and a half years at home, though ostensibly resting, his pen was not idle. It was during this interval that he translated the Church History and revised his commentaries on the New Testament.

Near the end of 1876, Dr. Stevens returned to Burma. He parted from his children and relatives in America, with the impression that he should see their faces no more. Not that he had a presentiment that the remainder of his career would be brief, but because he considered it extremely improbable that circumstances would ever make it desirable for him to return to his native land.

He at once applied himself to the routine of Mission work with as much zest and effectiveness, as if his age were two-score and two, instead of three-score and three.

In the spring of 1883, he suffered another of the attacks above referred to, and for a while, it seemed as if his work must be near its end. But from this he recovered, and, with his usual elasticity of temperament, resumed his labors, relinquishing only that part which would take him into the district where surgical help could not be obtained, when suddenly needed.

He was relieved, for a few months in 1880, of the pastoral care of the English Church, by the coming of Rev. W. R. Manley, and again in the latter part of the same year for a few months, by Rev. W. I. Price. He was not finally released, however, until the Rains of 1882. At that time, Dr. Cushing, in anticipation of the arrival of Rev. L. J. Denchfield in November as a permanent pastor, very kindly accepted the responsibility, and gave himself, with his well-known energy and tact, to the rallying of the Baptists, who had become scattered through the frequency of pastoral changes, and other causes.

The long, patient, and successful work of Dr. Stevens in connection with the English Baptist Church, dating from its formation in 1859, for twenty-three years, will make his name fragrant in the annals of that Church. The writer first became acquainted with the work of Dr. Stevens, in 1864, and at that time, the modest chapel at the corner of Merchant and Phayre Streets, in its crowded Sunday evening congregations, was a sight to give joy to angels. Between that time and 1881, two new congregations, the Presbyterian and the Methodist, were largely formed of those who had been habitual attendants upon Dr. Stevens' preaching, and yet the chapel continued to attract a goodly audience.

The Church membership was always small, but also, was always fluctuating, as had been that of the English Church in Maulmain, owing to a constantly changing military and mercantile community. Communities are rarely permanent in India. But in this way little colonies have established themselves in other places, from which other churches have grown. Conspicuous among these is the Baptist Church in Madras, which was formed when the 84th Regiment reached that place from Maulmain. General Sir David Russell, then Captain Russell, with a good number of privates in that regiment, was baptized by Mr. Stevens in 1843. These with other officers of the 84th Regiment, converted and baptized while in Burma, led in a movement to form a Baptist Church, and to build for it an edifice, for which latter, Captain Russell, being a man of some means, provided in large measure the requisite funds.

As an illustration of the value of this work among the English and of its subsequent advantage to the Burmese work itself, many years after, while serving in Canada as Commander-in-Chief of her Majesty's forces there, this same Sir David Russell, at a large meeting of representatives of Young Men's Christian Associations in the U.S.A. and Canada, which was held in Montreal, and over which he presided, took the opportunity to acknowledge his sense of personal indebtedness to the Christian effort of the American Missionaries in Burma ; and still further, in 1877, Sir David entrusted Dr. Stevens with the sum of Rs. 16,000, to be used for the support and training of native evangelists in Burma.*

Thus, though at any given period, the membership of the Rangoon Baptist Church was small, yet of many may it be said, " this and that man was born in her," and of many more, that in that humble building, the claims of the Gospel were by Dr. Stevens, for more than a score of years, tenderly, faithfully, and urgently laid before them.

While Dr. Stevens was preëminently a preaching missionary, he was not indifferent to the claims of education. As an auxiliary in evangelistic labor, and especially, as an indispensable condition of permanency and progress in the native churches, he always accorded a high place to schools of every grade. He felt himself, however, unable to personally engage in school work. The multiplicity of his engagements was a sufficient excuse for this apparent neglect. It was this, and no lack of interest, that he pleaded as his excuse for declining an invitation from Mr., now Sir Charles Bernard, to accept the position of vice-president of the Educational Syndicate, established in 1881. He did accept however, as less incompatible with his engagements, the office of president of the Board of Trustees of the Rangoon Baptist College, and in that institution, he always evinced a lively interest. Often

---

* This sum was used freely, during the life-time of Dr. Stevens, in both the Karen and Burmese departments, and the unexpended balance, invested in " Russell Place," was entrusted shortly before his death, to his son and son-in-law in Burma, to be used by them in accordance with the intention of the distinguished donor.

also, has the writer heard him, when returning from one of his stated preaching services in the Kemendine Girls' School, express his gratitude to God that there was such an institution in Burma, where hundreds of Burmese girls of both christian and heathen families, could be kept constantly under the elevating and sanctifying influences of christian training.

Although a Georgian by birth and warmly attached to the South, yet his sympathies extended over the whole of his beloved country. He loved the North and the South, and none rejoiced more than he, in the return of union between them in 1865, and in the extinction of the deplorable cause of the alienation which had existed between the two sections.

The separation of the Southern churches from the Baptist Triennial Convention in 1846, was a sore trial to him. Up to that time, he felt that at least a part of his commission and of his support, came from the churches of his own loved South. And this regret was mutual, for when at home in 1854-6, the secretary of the Southern Board, desirous of continuing to have a share in his support, and also in the Burmese mission, *their* first-love also in the Foreign work, offered to provide his salary and to allow him to retain his connection with Burma, and to work under the general direction of the Northern Board, provided that he could be counted among the missionaries of the Southern Board. The matter was referred to the secretary of the Northern Board ; but as it was feared that, in view of the dissatisfaction of a few missionaries about that time, for whom was formed the Free Mission Society, his leaving the Board at Boston might be misunderstood, the whole subject was dropped.

Towards the close of December 1885, he was attacked by what seemed to be a severe cold, but soon, more alarming symptoms manifested themselves, and medical help was summoned. It was on a Wednesday evening at dusk, the last Wednesday in the year, when the alarming announcement was made that the heart was seriously affected, and his condition critical. Well does the writer remember taking the sad tidings to the weekly Karen prayer-meeting which was at that moment assembling in the Seminary chapel, and asking that prayer should be offered for that valuable life. During the following months, much prayer was offered by his missionary associates at this and other stations, and by the churches of all the races who loved his name. So sudden was the breaking down at last, that on the following Friday, Dr. Stevens had promised to make the address in Burmese, at the New Year's day union meeting of all the congregations of Baptist Christians in Rangoon; and a half finished outline of a sermon, suited for the last Sabbath of the year, was lying on his desk, from the text, sadly, and yet, for this good and faithful steward, not sadly significant, " Give an account of thy stewardship, for thou mayest be no longer steward."

Though sudden to those about him, Dr. Stevens had felt the heart difficulty growing upon him for a year or more, so that he was not wholly unprepared for the decision in which the three doctors consulted concurred, that his active work was done. It was still hoped however, by his friends, that by the extreme quiet which was almost the only thing which the physicians could prescribe, his usefulness might be prolonged at his study table if not elsewhere. At times, from January till June, he had intervals when he was quite comfortable, and his children in America could be cheered by the tidings of improvement; but each attack left him weaker than its predecessor, and all around him felt that he was nearing heaven. Yet his own hopefulness continued until June 14th, when he for the first time said, " I am going." "It was at the close of a day of great suffering," writes his daughter, "a continual struggle for breath. We supposed he would never speak or recognize us again, when he broke forth into a long, earnest, beautiful prayer, much of it clothed in the language of Scripture. He commenced by saying how gladly he would continue in his much loved work; 'I have served Thee a long time, but if Thou sayest it is enough, Thy will be done.' Then he prayed for this household. 'Bless us as individuals; bless us as a household; grant that every one, *every one*, may be wholly consecrated, *wholly consecrated, wholly consecrated*, to the service of the Lord.' He prayed for his children and grandchildren that all, *everyone*, might learn the joy of leading souls to Christ, and that they might esteem His service of higher honor than any possible earthly honor. 'The world does not so regard Thy service; but we are not of the world.'—He remembered Burma. 'Up there, all will be of one mind, *of one mind*, and that the mind of Christ,' and closed with uttering strong assurances in Scripture language, of the ultimate triumph of that ' Name, which is above every name.' He reiterated with great fervor the plea of Moses, which he had urged many times before, ' For the glory of Thy name,' repeating that phrase, ' His name, for the honor of His name, to the glory of His name.' He spoke some endearing words to mother, taking her hand, and then added, ' I am going.' After a little, his mind seemed to wander, and he said, ' It must be time to go to bed; let us have prayers,' and turning to Mr. Freiday, whose tender night-watchings during that eventful week, are gratefully remembered, he requested that he would offer prayer."

This memorable prayer seemed the more remarkable to his family from the fact that it was his first audible prayer, since 1886 had commenced. The weakness of his voice, and the violent agitation of his heart, caused by speaking more than a few words at a time, had deprived him and his family of the privilege he and they had ever so much enjoyed.

" On Tuesday evening," Mrs. Smith's letter continues, " when the Seminary students sang in their evening worship at the chapel, dear father aroused, and said, ' How sweet such sounds in a land like this.' The hymn, the strains of which came floating into the chamber of sickness, was the beautiful one entitled, ' It is well with my soul.' "

Wednesday, Thursday and Friday passed; loving hands of his own family and of missionary friends, ministered to his wants; but these were few. He slept heavily, and it was difficult to arouse him sufficiently to take needed refreshment. His work was ended, his last word had been spoken, his last prayer offered. Early on Saturday A.M., of the 19th day of June, his failing pulse indicated the near approach of the great change, and at 4.45, just at break of day, his pure spirit took its flight. We bowed around his couch, while Mr. Brayton, his fellow voyager in the "*Rosabella*" nearly fifty years before, and his dear and life-long friend, led our hearts in prayer to the " Father of mercies and God of all comfort."

Early in the morning of the first day of the week, after a brief service at the house, conducted by Rev. Mr. Brayton, at the tolling of the Seminary chapel bell and the bell of the adjoining S. P. G. S. John's College, the funeral cortege wended its way through the thronged and busy city, passing the Burmese chapel at Lammadau, whose walls were never more to echo to the sound of his voice, and on to the English Baptist Church, where a dense congregation awaited the obsequies. Devout men tenderly bore him into the Church. The services, which were conducted in the Burmese and English languages, commenced with the singing in Burmese of the hymn, a translation of which was made by Dr. Stevens for the funeral of Ko En, for many years pastor of the Burmese Church,

> " Servant of God, well done!
> Rest from thy loved employ;
> The battle fought, the victory won,
> Enter thy Master's joy!"

This hymn was most beautifully and feelingly rendered by a choir composed of a selection of Burmese girls from the Kemendine Girls' School, where he had so often preached, and was followed by the reading, interspersed with remarks, of a choice selection of Scripture passages by Rev. Dr. Rose, and prayer by Ko Shway Oung, an aged Burmese preacher, for many years associated with Dr. Stevens in Christian work.

The services were continued with an affectionate address in English, by Rev. L. J. Denchfield, the pastor, on the words, "And they took up the body and buried it; and went and told Jesus."

After the services in the Church, the body was accompanied by a vast concourse to the cemetery, where repose so many of the sainted missionary dead; Wade, and Mason, and Ingalls, and Bennett, and others, for many years associated with him in work; and now to be together in the repose of death, until the morning of the Resurrection. There too, for many years, have reposed the ashes of two little girls, his dear grandchildren; and all around, are the graves of those of many races, to whom he ministered in life, as pastor and friend.

We laid him away in full and joyful hope of a blessed resurrection.

Little, in respect to Dr. Stevens' character, remains to be added to what has already been indicated. When, at his funeral, Dr. Rose, in his Burmese address, referred to the description of Barnabas in Acts xi. 24., as summarizing for us in a few words the character of Dr. Stevens, the appropriateness of the reference received the assent of the congregation. "He was a good man and full of the Holy Ghost, and of faith."

He was a man of prayer. He spent much time in prayer. Secret prayer was his delight; and on two occasions in his life, the Lord was pleased to reveal Himself to him in an overwhelming manner. He could never refer to those two Bethel experiences, without the deepest emotion. Much of the sweetness and evenness of his temper and life, were due to those seasons of daily communion with his Saviour, with which no engagements were allowed to interfere. He was fond of social prayer and of the place of public worship. The stated seasons of worship, whether on the Sabbath or week days, whether the worship was conducted in a known or unknown tongue, were sacredly observed by him, throughout his entire life. He felt that even where he could not join intelligently in the worship, by his presence he indicated his sympathy with the object of the service, and he was unwilling to forego a single opportunity of showing his attachment to Christ, and his love for the ordinances of Christ's house.

He believed in the benefit of association in Christian work, and in the communion of the saints. He was the father of associational gatherings in Burma, being, we are informed, the originator in 1843, of the old Maulmain Karen and Burmese Association.

The Pegu Association, which included all the Burmese Churches on the Rangoon side of the Gulf of Martaban, owed its origin to him, in 1860. The annual gatherings of this Association he greatly enjoyed, and while in the country, was never absent, until at the last one in Henthada, in February of this year. He sent to it, however, his Christian greeting, and was present in spirit, though absent in body. How much he was missed, and how affectionately he was remembered, is pleasantly described by Dr. Jameson in a published letter, from which a single paragraph is taken.

" Our senior missionary to the Burmans, Dr. Stevens of Rangoon, who has always attended the meetings of the Association, was, this year, not only unable to be present, but was confined to his bed at home, in very feeble health. I asked one native brother whether he was enjoying himself. He said he was ; but he missed Dr. Stevens all the time. While a motion was being made to unite in special prayer for Dr. Stevens and Mrs. Bennett, also in infirm health, a telegram arrived, with a salutation from Dr. Stevens, and an appropriate Scripture reference, 1 Cor. 15 : 58, ' Therefore, my beloved brethren, be ye steadfast, unmovable, always abounding in the work of the Lord, forasmuch as ye know that your labor is not in vain in the Lord.' The attention of the meeting was called to the great debt of the Burman Christians to Dr. Stevens, in view of his valuable commentaries on different books of the Bible, which are such a means of spiritual knowledge to many scattered disciples, who have no missionary or native preacher to explain to them the word of God. We united in prayer as proposed, and sent a telegram with a reference to 3rd John, 2, ' Beloved, I wish above all things, that thou mayest prosper and be in health, even as thy soul prospereth.' "

He was one of the constituent members of the Burma Baptist Missionary Convention, and was more often elected to the office of president of that body, than any other man. His urbanity, his impartiality, his patience, his animation, and his superb command of the Burmese language, made him a favorite presiding officer. At the same time, he was destitute of all *desire* for pre-eminence. He seemed unaware of his own excellencies, and accepted offices not as distinctions, but as opportunities for greater usefulness, which he dared not refuse.

Another characteristic of Dr. Stevens was his " diligence in business, serving the Lord." He carefully gathered up remnants of time, for extra toils. Some work or other was always on hand, with which to fill up the interstices. His was a busy life. When at Mergui, in 1844, for a few months, on account of sickness in his family, he studied and reduced to writing the language of the Salongs. As already referred to, when at home in 1874-76, he prepared several important works in the Burmese language. Constituted as he was, rest for him, was change of employment.

He had no time therefore to brood over misfortunes, fancied or real. This contributed to the cheerfulness of his disposition, and that again to the health given him in such large measure, throughout his long career. The latter was promoted also by the regular exercise, consisting principally in morning and evening walks, which he commenced while at College, and conscientiously kept up, to the last year of his life.

Dr. Stevens had much of " the grace" of liberality. From principle, a tenth of his income was always set apart, and from the remaining nine-tenths also, he indulged his generous soul in quiet, unostentatious giving. Nor was he backward in his efforts to develop the same grace in the churches committed to his oversight. Much grief did he feel that the native Christians did not more fully emulate their heathen neighbors ; yet he had reason to rejoice that to a large extent, they responded to the calls made upon them, in connection with Christian work for themselves and the heathen around them. The liberality of the Burmese Church in Rangoon, bears testimony to the soundness of his views on self-support. For many years, besides the support of its own pastor and current Church expenses, they pensioned a superannuated pastor, repaired and kept in order their Chapel, and sustained an evangelist at Pegu, until a Church was gathered there, large enough to provide for its own support, when the evangelist received ordination and was settled as pastor of the newly formed Church, and the Rangoon Church turned its attention to a similar work in another heathen community. At his instance, the Rangoon Missionary Society was formed, to receive contributions which he was in the habit of of soliciting from the English speaking community ; and through this society, many evangelists and Bible women have been supported in Christian work, among the heathen. It is peculiarly pleasant to give this testimony to Dr. Stevens' successful efforts in training disciples in the habit of self-support, because of the impression which has been created by recently published Tracts, that self-supporting Christian communities are limited to the Karen department of the Missions in Burma. It should be added also that Dr. Stevens was not alone in this, others of his brethren, who labor among the Burmans, having been equally successful.

The consistency and rigidness with which he held his distinctive views as a strict Baptist, not infrequently gave offence, and, perhaps, sometimes alienated from him those, whose views were more elastic. This would grieve, but could not move him. Loyalty to the truth made him firm, while the example and words of the apostle both cheered and confirmed him, " For if I yet pleased men, I should not be a servant of Christ." At the same time he was destitute of all bitterness of feeling towards those who differed with him. He gave them full credit for conscientiousness, and thanked God for the good that he could find and enjoy in them. This great charity combined with unyielding adherence to what he conceived to be the mind of Christ, was happily illustrated in the difficulties in the Burmese Church under his care, which clouded the last year of his life. The adoption of " premillennial views," he did not regard as a cause for Church discipline. His own views at one period in his life, were premillennial. His chief objection to them, in addition to their believed unsoundness, was that the principles of interpretation, which are relied upon to justify those views, make it easy for the unlearned and unstable to adopt other doctrines, which are positively pernicious in their tendencies and results. Further specification is unnecessary ; but it is believed that these errors of interpretation are by none more deeply regretted, than by premillennial leaders, whose higher mental and spiritual discipline, enable them to preserve the due proportion of truth. These distortions of interpretation, persistently held and offensively urged upon others, led to a schism in the Burmese Church ; but for those erring ones, Dr. Stevens ever felt the tenderest pity. " I have nourished and brought up children," he used sometimes sorrowfully to say of them, " and they have rebelled against me."

In the evangelistic work of other Christian denominations, he ever felt the liveliest interest. When the Methodists commenced their work in Rangoon, he opened the Baptist chapel to Dr. Thoburn for his preaching services, and rejoiced in the hopeful conversions which resulted. He was glad, when the Presbyterians felt strong enough to attempt an independent church work, although thereby, the Baptist chapel lost some of its most constant and intelligent attendants.

He rejoiced in the school and church work of the S. P. G. Missionaries, and expressed his thankfulness for the work of the Roman Catholics, in view of some of the cardinal truths of our religion, which are disseminated by them.

In 1864, Brown University, his Alma Mater conferred upon him the degree of Doctor of Divinity, a degree which he was too modest either to seek or to decline.

Dr. Stevens' Missionary life in Burma covered a period of forty eight years and three months. Gladly would he, if permitted, have toiled on, another decade. He had strong faith in the ultimate victory which was to crown the labors of Christ's servants, in this and all heathen lands. However untoward present circumstances might be, he would not, could not be discouraged. His face was ever toward the sun-rising. His eye was fixed upon the Star of Bethlehem, and that, to him, was the Morning Star of the millennial day. He looked wistfully at the door which opened into Upper Burma on the first day of January, 1886; and though it then seemed to those about him a vain hope, yet, less than a month before his departure, his face pale with weakness but lighted up with the energy of hope, he exclaimed, " Who knows ? I may yet be permitted to preach in Mandalay !"

And until the autumn of 1885, it might well have been anticipated that this would be his privilege. One who listened to his last sermon in the Burmese Chapel at Lammadau, near the close of that year, remembers thinking at the time, " how strong and clear that voice ! How full of promise for years to come !" Until the last six months of weakness and suffering, his hair had become but slightly silvered, and his step had lost but little of its elasticity, nor had his manners lost any of his life-long thoughtful attention to the graceful amenities of family and social life.

" He rests from his labors." But it is the kind of rest he took on earth ; a change of work. There " they rest not day and night."

By loving hands, a palm has been planted at the foot of his grave, fit emblem for one whose life of cheerful, hopeful toil and conflict, is crowned at length with the victor's joy.

As a fitting completion of these pages, we may quote as applicable to the life thus briefly and imperfectly sketched, the closing sentences in the remarks of Dr. H. M. King, to the memory of Dr. Ripley, whom Dr. Stevens ever regarded as a second father, and whom, in character, he remarkably resembled.

"He was one of the purest, gentlest, saintliest of men, endowed richly with that love which vaunteth not itself, is not puffed up, doth not behave itself unseemly, seeketh not her own, is not easily provoked, thinketh no evil. Humbly and without ostentation, he filled the honorable place which Providence assigned to him. His spirit showed an unmistakable and beautiful likeness to Him with Whom he lived in constant communion. He seemed ever to move in the atmosphere of heaven. His smile was a perpetual benediction. His peaceful end was the fitting termination of a life which was pervaded with the calm and sanctifying trust of the Gospel of Christ. Few have been taken from the scenes of earth to the abodes of the redeemed, who have been so completely clad in the ' robe of readiness.' "

"Of such as he was, there be few on earth ;
Of such as he is, there be many in heaven ;
And life is all the sweeter that he lived ;
And all he loved more sacred for his sake ;
And death is all the brighter that he died ;
And heaven is all the happier that he's there."

Since the above sketch went to Press, the attention of the writer has been drawn to a copy of the "Minutes of the Sixteenth Anniversary of the Georgia Baptist Convention, held at Ruckersville, Georgia, on the 5th, 6th, and 8th of May 1837," from which the following extract is made.

"*Sabbath morning, May 7.*

This was a solemn day, and forms an *important era* in the history of this body. In conformity to previous notice, a large congregation assembled at 9 o'clock in the Baptist Church, to witness the ordination of our beloved brother, Edward A. Stevens, as a Minister of the Gospel and a Missionary to the perishing heathen, in compliance with the request of the Sunbury Baptist Church. It was a deeply interesting occasion; every heart seemed to be affected, and when this *devoted* youth presented himself before the Presbytery, almost every eye wept, and the breathing of many pious souls was poured forth that the blessings of God might abide with him at home, amid the dangers of the ocean, and in the dreary and desolate field for which he is destined.

The sermon was delivered by Elder J. Mercer, from Luke 6 : 39, 40, 'Can the blind lead the blind,' etc. The examination was conducted by Elder V. R. Thornton. It was clear and entirely satisfactory, both in relation to Christian Experience, and the motives which influenced him, doctrine and qualifications. The charge was given by Elder I. L. Brooks, of South Carolina. Prayer by Elder C. D. Mallary, and the right hand of fellowship by Elder A. T. Holmes."

Printed by Libri Plureos GmbH in Hamburg, Germany